D1537414

LYN-Z ADAMS HAWKINS PASTRANA

EXTREME SPORTS STARS

BY MATT SCHEFF

SportsZone

An Imprint of Abdo Publishing
www.abdopublishing.com

www.abdopublishing.com

Published by Abdo Publishing, a division of ABDO, PO Box 398166, Minneapolis, Minnesota 55439. Copyright © 2015 by Abdo Consulting Group, Inc. International copyrights reserved in all countries. No part of this book may be reproduced in any form without written permission from the publisher. SportsZone™ is a trademark and logo of Abdo Publishing.

Printed in the United States of America, North Mankato, Minnesota
042014
092014

Cover Photos: Paul A. Hebert/Invision/AP Images (foreground); Mark J. Terrill/AP Images (background)
Interior Photos: Josh Chapel/ZUMA Press/Newscom, 1, 11; Cody York Photography, 4-5, 18-19, 26, 30 (right); Tony Donaldson/Icon SMI, 6, 9, 20-21, 22; Kevin Sullivan/ZUMA Press/Newscom, 7; Miles Chrisinger/Icon SMI, 8, 23; Dennis Van Tine/ABACAUSA.COM/Newscom, 10; Laura Embry/U-T San Diego/ZUMA Press/Newscom, 12-13; Evan Hurd/Corbis, 14-15, 16-17; Mark J. Terrill/AP Images, 24-25; Steve Helber/AP Images, 27, 30 (left); Philip Scott Andrews/AP Images, 28-29, 31

Editor: Chrös McDougall
Series Designer: Maggie Villaume

Library of Congress Control Number: 2014932905

Cataloging-in-Publication Data
Scheff, Matt.
 Lyn-Z Adams Hawkins Pastrana / Matt Scheff.
   p. cm. -- (Extreme sports stars)
Includes index.
ISBN 978-1-62403-454-1
1. Pastrana, Lyn-Z Adams Hawkins, 1989- --Juvenile literature.
2. Skateboarders--United States--Biography--Juvenile literature.
I. Title.
796.22/092--dc23
[B]
                                    2014932905

CONTENTS

Lyn-Z flies through the air at the 2010 X Games.

FAST FACT

Lyn-Z's nicknames include "Lil Girl," "L-Hawk," and "Punky Brewster."

THE 540 McTWIST

The 2009 Quiksilver Tony Hawk Show in Paris, France, was a big party. Thousands of fans jammed to music and enjoyed a show by some of the world's best skateboarders. Many fans came to see the skateboarding legend Tony Hawk. But almost everyone went home talking about rising star Lyn-Z Adams Hawkins.

Lyn-Z took her turn in the halfpipe. She built up some speed. Then she launched herself into the air. Lyn-Z grabbed her board and spun one and a half times in the air. She landed safely. It was a 540 McTwist! No female had ever done that trick before. Lyn-Z fell to her knees in celebration. All of the other skateboarders ran to celebrate with her at the bottom of the ramp. She had just made skateboarding history.

Lyn-Z shows off her gold medal at the 2009 X Games.

In 2012, twelve-year-old Alana Smith became the second female to land the 540 McTwist.

Lyn-Z flips through the air in 2012.

Lyn-Z rides at the 2009 Skateboarding World Championships.

EARLY LIFE

Lindsey Adams Hawkins was born September 21, 1989, in San Diego, California. As a child, Lindsey got tired of writing out her full name. So she started writing Lyn-Z instead. She told her mom about wanting to change her name. Her mom agreed that Lyn-Z sounded like a cool name.

Lyn-Z's mother ran a bed and breakfast in Mexico. So her family spent half of their time there and the other half in California.

Lyn-Z warms up for a demo at the 2002 X Games.

Lyn-Z was a natural athlete. She played soccer and basketball. She was also a swimmer and a diver. She learned to surf at age five. Her older brother Tyler was a good skateboarder. When Lyn-Z was six, Tyler taught her how to skateboard. They skated together at a local sports club.

Lyn-Z, right, poses with fellow athletes, from left, Chanelle Sladics, Grete Eliassen, and Elena Hight at the Salute to Women in Sports Gala in 2012.

Lyn-Z competes at the 2010 X Games.

FAST FACT

Lyn-Z was taking part in surfing competitions by age nine. She still enjoys surfing today.

Lyn-Z enjoyed riding her skateboard. But she didn't get serious about skateboarding until around age ten. She started entering competitions. At first, she didn't really understand what to do. In her first event, she left after her first run. She didn't even know that she was supposed to do a second run!

Lyn-Z skates in a skate pool at age 14.

FAST FACT

Other skateboarders noticed Lyn-Z's talent. Growing up, she even practiced with skateboarding legend Tony Hawk.

Lyn-Z skates on a vert ramp in 2003.

RISING STAR

In 2001, Lyn-Z entered a contest called the All Girl Skate Jam. She won first place in the amateur division. Then she did it again in 2002. At age 13, she was already one of the rising stars in girls' skateboarding.

Lyn-Z does a rail trick in 2003.

16

In 2003, the X Games held women's skateboarding events for the first time. Fourteen-year-old Lyn-Z took the silver medal in the park event and the bronze in the vert event. But 2003 was also a year of tragedy for Lyn-Z. Her father passed away. She missed him terribly.

FAST FACT

Lyn-Z decorates her own boards. She writes RIP (for Rest in Peace) on many of them as a way to honor her dad.

BREAKING NEW GROUND

Lyn-Z really made her mark at the 2004 X Games. Her best run in the vert event was unlike any other. She did one hard trick after the next. The crowd gasped as she did a kick flip indy grab. While spinning in the air, she kicked her board, caught it, and then landed on it. No woman had ever landed that trick in a competition before. The great run earned Lyn-Z her first X Games gold medal.

Lyn-Z flies through the air during the vert competition at the 2007 X Games.

Lyn-Z suffered a terrible fall in 2005. She hurt her head and broke her arm in two places. But she wasn't willing to miss the X Games. So she skated with a cast on her arm! She amazed the fans by taking the silver medal in vert.

Lyn-Z rides in the 2005 X Games with a broken arm.

FAST FACT

Lyn-Z was the first woman to successfully jump the giant DC Mega Ramp. She sailed 55 feet (16.8 m) from the launch point to the landing point!

Lyn-Z stands atop the medal stand after winning the women's vert at the 2009 X Games.

FAST FACT

Skateboarding is Lyn-Z's best sport. But she has also entered snowboarding and surfing competitions.

Los Angel

In 2006, Lyn-Z hurt her knee while snowboarding. She missed the X Games that year. But she came back strong in 2007 to win gold in vert. Then in 2009, she won the X Games vert for a third time. She also won the vert event at the Skateboarding World Championships.

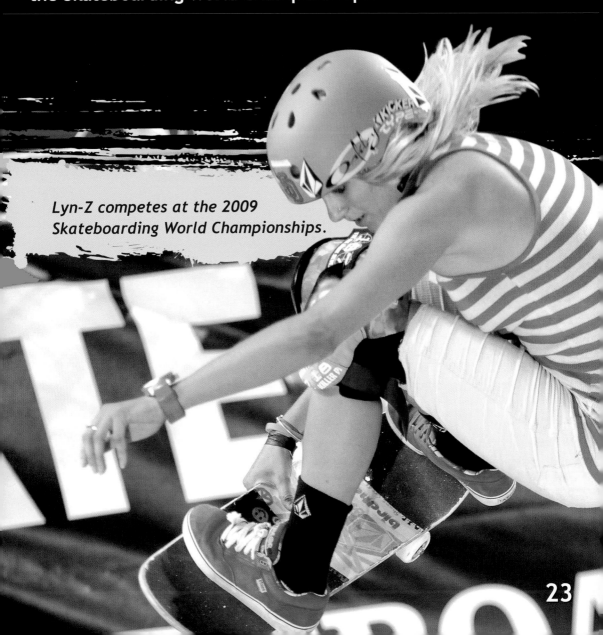

Lyn-Z competes at the 2009 Skateboarding World Championships.

ACTION SPORTS POWER COUPLE

Lyn-Z was at the top of her sport when she met fellow extreme sports star Travis Pastrana. He did motocross and NASCAR racing in addition to performing stunts. A friend introduced Lyn-Z to Travis at the X Games. Lyn-Z and Travis soon fell in love. In 2011, Travis proposed to Lyn-Z in front of a crowd at a Las Vegas show called Nitro Circus Live. Lyn-Z said yes, and the couple was married later that year.

Travis Pastrana pulls off a double backflip during the moto x best trick event at the 2006 X Games.

Lyn-Z competes in skateboard vert at the 2010 X Games.

FAST FACT

Lyn-Z was a character in the 2006 video game *Tony Hawk's Project 8*. She was just the second woman to be featured in the popular series of games.

Travis and Lyn-Z were the most famous couple in action sports. They traveled around the country to cheer each other on. In early 2013, Lyn-Z found out that she would have to take some time off from competing. She was going to have a baby! The couple welcomed a little girl, Addy, on September 2, 2013.

Lyn-Z and Travis pose for a picture before a 2012 stock car race.

Lyn-Z remains one of the biggest stars in pro skateboarding.

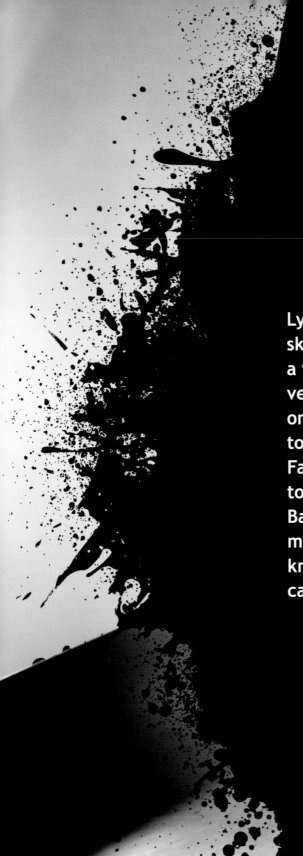

Lyn-Z doesn't plan to stop skating just because she has a family. She got back on a vert ramp for the first time on November 1, 2013. She told her friends and fans on Facebook that it felt good to be upside down again! Balancing a family with skating might be hard. But those who know Lyn-Z believe that she can pull it off.

TIMELINE

1989

Lyn-Z is born on September 21 in San Diego, California.

1995

Lyn-Z's brother Tyler teaches her how to skateboard.

2001

Lyn-Z takes first place in the amateur division at the All Girl Skate Jam.

2003

At age 14, Lyn-Z wins two medals in the X Games.

2004

Lyn-Z lands a kick flip indy grab and wins the 2004 X Games vert gold medal.

2009

Lyn-Z becomes the first woman to land a 540 McTwist.

2011

Lyn-Z marries fellow action sports star Travis Pastrana.

2013

Lyn-Z announces that she is going to have a baby. She gives birth to a daughter, Addy, in September.

GLOSSARY

amateur
A person who is not paid to compete in a sport.

halfpipe
A U-shaped ramp used in skateboarding and other sports.

indy
A trick in which the skater grabs the toe side of the skateboard with his or her back hand.

McTwist
A trick in which the skater spins 540 degrees to the backside while performing a mute grab.

motocross
Off-road races on motorcycles.

street
In skateboarding, an event in which skateboarders do tricks on a variety of obstacles, including ramps and railings.

vert
Short for vertical; in skateboarding, vert is a type of event held on a halfpipe with tall, vertical walls.

31

INDEX